Strategic Warfare
The Pursuit of God's Glory

Strategic Warfare

The Pursuit of God's Glory

Author: Elder Sarina D. Hardison
Edited By: Bryan Brown

Order this book online at www.trafford.com
or email orders@trafford.com

Most Trafford titles are also available at major online book retailers.

Printed in Victoria, BC, Canada.

ISBN: 978-1-4269-2989-2 (sc)

ISBN: 978-1-4269-2988-5 (e-book)

*Our mission is to efficiently provide the world's finest, most comprehensive book publishing
service, enabling every author to experience success. To find out how to publish your book, your
way, and have it available worldwide, visit us online at www.trafford.com*

Trafford rev. 3/22/2010

www.trafford.com

North America & international
toll-free: 1 888 232 4444 (USA & Canada)
phone: 250 383 6864 ♦ fax: 812 355 4082

Dedication

All glory to God for teaching me how to live strategically and not haphazardly, for loving me when I struggled to love myself, and for looking passed my faults, and seeing my needs. I love you for your faithfulness and appreciate you for your holiness. Thank you father!

To my son, Treviaun, thank you for putting up with me through this process of writing this book. I love you with all my heart! You are truly a blessing sent from God to me. Stay encouraged and be blessed. It's your inheritance.

To my family: Mom, Dad, Camillya, Artrese, Aletha, Desmond and Michael thank you for the support of a strong family. I love you all. You are greatly appreciated!

To all my nieces and nephews: Stephon, Dezalyn, Nia, Jaiel, Jaylon, Michael Jr., Amya, and Jeremiah I love you all so much. Keep walking in childlike faith and be blessed. Your childlike faith is your door to inherit that which God has promised you!

To Pastor Don Allen Henson Sr. thank you for your encouragement in writing this book. You are greatly loved and appreciated. May God bless and keep you as you walk in the anointing given to you by God for such a time as this.

Acknowledgements

Apostle Arthur C. Hardison III, thank you for building me up in the unadulterated Word of God and for living the Word line upon line and precept upon precept. I honor the God in you man of God.

Pastor Sabrina A. Hardison, thank you for your words of wisdom and unfailing love. Your influence will never be forgotten. Keep walking in your anointing woman of God.

Elder Cris A. Ward, you are a man of God to be honored for your faithfulness to God and in the eyes of the people. You have truly impacted my life. Be blessed man of God.

Works of Deliverance Fellowship International Ministries Family, I love you all and I acknowledge you for your faithfulness to God and your support one for another. Be blessed family.

Breath of God Christian fellowship Family, I love you all; and I thank you for being the awesome family you are. God bless you.

Maranatha Christian Fellowship family you are all greatly loved and appreciated. Stay committed and walk in the anointing of God. Be blessed!

To every affiliate of the Kingdom of God, be encouraged to walk in your anointing not haphazardly. Let us walk strategically as we wage war on the enemy.

Foreword

This book Strategic Warfare sets a standard and design for the one who is mindful of the fight. Even the scriptures teach us to put on the whole armor of God, and though it seems as if the life of Christ is unrealized reading this book you'll come to an understanding of what it means to live in Christ. For the warfare is in the mind and in the heart and the word must be permitted to examine the contents of each place, causing the thoughts and heart to line up, if the rest will ever be applied. This book will motivate the parts of you that are not living but will teach you how to fight how to live and how to stand.

To God is all the glory!!!!!!

Apostle Arthur C. Hardison III

Introduction

In warfare, God wants his people to move strategically and not haphazardly. Having the knowledge of Christ but denying his power is like electricity that powers a house being cut loose and its power becoming deadly to everyone it meets. It still has its power, but the power cannot effectively be used for its purpose throughout the house, because it lacks direction. (Hebrews 4:11-13 NKJV) literally tells us how the word which is our instructions to being pleasing to God discovers our condition. It reads; *Let us therefore be diligent to enter that rest, lest anyone fall according to the same example of disobedience, for the word of God is living and powerful and sharper than any two-edged sword, piercing even to the division of the soul and spirit and of joints and marrow and is a discerner of the thoughts and intents of the heart. And there is no creature hidden from his sight, but all things are naked and opened to the eyes of him to whom we must give an account.* Now in verse 11 it encourages us to be diligent which translates into the words determined and relentless in which we must be to enter into that rest which only comes by applying the word of God to our lives and in living it we come to find that, that rest consist of righteousness, peace and joy in the Lord *(Romans 14:17 NKJV)* In order to know how to live right, to have peace in every situation, and to stay in joy we must follow the instructions of the word given to us by God. A soldier with fatigues, boots, grenades, and a gun doesn't make him fit for battle, It is the training and the skillful use of the weapons used in battle that teaches him how to defeat his enemy, not on his own strength but under the instruction of his command-in-chief. To function strategically in pursuit of Gods glory, we must realize that there are three basic elements of warfare: Mobility, Fire-power, and Security. The use of all three can and will empower you to run after and obtain the glory of God.

Contents

Chapter One

Mobility

Mobility is the ability to move strategically by following instructions. The strategic movement that I am talking about comes from that of the Holy Spirit, when we as the people of God begin to move strategically according to the will of the Father for our lives, it is in this place that we begin to see, namely the power of God. *(Acts 1:3-5 NKJV) says During the forty days after his crucifixion, he appeared to the apostles from time to time, and he proved to them in many ways that he was actually alive. And he talked to them about the Kingdom of God. Once when he was eating with them he commanded them, do not leave Jerusalem until the Father sends you the gift he promised, as I told you before. John Baptized with water, but in just a few days you will be baptized with the Holy Spirit.*

Now mobility functions by obedience. Had the disciples left Jerusalem before they received the gifts of the Holy Spirit

and went out preaching and teaching what Jesus taught them they would have just been flowing haphazardly, why? Because they had the knowledge of Christ, but if they lacked obedience there they would lack direction thus lacking power. (Acts 1:8 NKJV) But you will receive power when the Holy Spirit comes upon you. And you will be my witnesses, telling people about me everywhere in Jerusalem, throughout Judea, in Samaria, and to the ends of the earth.

What are the gifts of the Holy Spirit? And why are they important before we can tell someone else about the goodness of Jesus?

The gifts of the Spirit are best quoted or explained as "beyond what we as humans can imagine." (Isaiah 11:1-5 NKJV) speaks about the gifts in their form of Wisdom, and Understanding, The spirit of Counsel and Might, the Spirit of Knowledge, and the fear of the Lord. Without these gifts the disciples would have been going out in man's knowledge or wisdom, which lacks the direction and substance that only comes from God. We as the people of God have to see that we don't know the way without the leading of the Holy Spirit, We will constantly make a mess of things, consequently having why it was so vital for the disciples to wait on the Holy Spirit and His gifts to empower them to do the will of the Father. This leads us to another part of strategic warfare through mobility, Waiting. You may ask the question how can I be mobile which is moving, and be waiting which means to stand still? Well if you remember that the mobility in which we speak of in strategic warfare, is the ability to move according to instructions and then take into account the actions through obedience, and the Holy Spirits leading *(Acts 1:3-5NKJV) ,We must be instant in season and out of season (2 Timothy 4:2 NKJV)*

(Instant **Meaning)** happening quickly without thought. Paul told Timothy to stir up his gift not because the use of it was upon him, but because he wanted him to be ready. We as the people of God must stay ready at all times. Sometimes we sleep on the enemy causing us not to think about this life as warfare, but the devil is always dressed and ready for war, it's what he does. His aim is to kill, still and to destroy, but we must be ready because the side in which we fight for comes to give life and that more abundantly Samson was ready for war, but he got cocky and in the midst of him being cocky he got carried away by the lust of his flesh. *(Judges 16 NKJV)* Samson was mobile but the lust of his eyes, the lust of his flesh and the pride of his life carried him to defeat, why? Instead of him using the wisdom of the Holy Spirit he leaned to his own understanding. All he seen is Delilah and not the trap of the enemy. In mobility, it is necessary for us to focus our eyes according to the Father, so we see what he sees. Yes all have sinned and come short of the glory of God, but that's no reason to live defeated. If we pull ourselves together, get focused, and understand that we are more than conquers by Christ Jesus and as we take on the blood of Jesus and abide in his blood, we will be redeemed from the hand of the enemy, our sins forgiven and our lives restored. Even now Lord, I decree and declare that I and the people of God would get up, shake off that which happened in our past, and move forward with

your will and plan in mind! I take authority over every spirit of self pity that would try to hold us in captivity, every spirit of hopelessness that would try to discourage, every spirit of perversion that would try to distort the plan of God in our lives. Satan I disarm you now in the name of Jesus, to drop your weapons back up and bow down! I speak deliverance where there is captivity, strength where there is weakness, and joy wear there is sorrow, in the name of Jesus, I claim every soul reading this book, for the Kingdom of God! That they would be delivered, set free, and made whole, in the matchless name of Jesus. AMEN. Let it be so.

(Hebrews 12:1, 2 NLT) Therefore since we are surrounded by such a huge crowd of witnesses to the life of faith, let us strip off every weight that slows us down, especially the sin that so easily trips us up. And let us run with endurance the race God has set before us. We do this by keeping our eye's on Jesus, the champion who initiates and perfects our faith, because of the joy awaiting him he endured the cross disregarding its shame, now he is seated in the place of honor beside God's throne.

People of God the battle has begun, as it has always been, but the devil is playing for keeps. We are in the final stretch and he knows his time is short so if he can get you to stop being mobile he knows that he will have opportunity to speak into your ear bringing you to a place of captivity.

There is one temptation that can overtake you that is common to man and that temptation is formed through your desires. I encourage you to check your desires at the door. Yes God said that he would give you the desires of your heart, but if your desires take precedence over the will of God, you defeat yourself. Samson's desires took hold of him because he desired Delilah and it led him to his defeat even though God being the faithful God He is, gave him one more chance to defeat his enemies, Sampson's defeat was still death, because he was overtaken by his desires. To be overtaken is to be consumed, so come on and let God get the glory out of your life! He wants the best for you.

<u>Receive Salvation</u>

If you are reading this chapter and have not receive Christ as your Lord and Savior, nor received his Holy Spirit now is the time. We are truly in the last days and Jesus is soon to return for his bride (the true believer).Your life is worth more than partying, drinking, and sexing it up. God has a plan for you, and your life is worth living. Please don't believe the religious lie that if you have been baptized by water you are on your way to heaven. You must be baptized in the redemptive blood of Jesus Christ, where there is forgiveness of all sins. There is no sin greater than the other, but there is eternal life in the blood. Receive him today; don't let it be said too late.

(Romans 10:9-10 NLT) – If you confess with your mouth that Jesus is Lord and believe in your heart that God raised him from the dead you will be saved. For it is by believing in your heart that you are made right by God and it is by confessing with your mouth that you are saved. Take this scripture as your own and pray this prayer with me: Father in the name of Jesus, I confess that I am a sinner and I ask that you would forgive me of my sinful ways. Today I receive you as my Lord and Savior. Please forgive me as I choose this day to abide in your blood for ever. Lord create in me a clean heart and renew a right spirit within me, and give me the strength to serve you everyday. I'll be so careful to give you all the glory and honor, in Jesus' Name Thank you for your grace and mercy AMEN. Let it be so.

Now if you prayed that prayer you are saved! Welcome to the family, now your job is to get into a Bible based church, one that preaches and teaches the unadulterated word. Read your Bible, pray and be free from the guilt and the shame of your past.

Forgive yourself, for whom the Son sets free is free indeed.

Chapter Two

Fire Power

Fire-power is based on the capacity to deliver. It is the endurance of the man, while mobility says move obediently, fire – power says move and don't stop, endure regardless of the obstacle. Some obstacles we put there, while others are there to test our faith. One thing that I found out the hard way is that when you start moving you do not stop regardless of the distraction. Distractions cause you to look back and for every time you look back, a sacrifice occurs, whether it is in your finances, your health, your children, or whatever the case may be. The word is true when it says, obedience is better than sacrifice. I've come to learn that I would rather be obedient than to lose out on the blessings of God it's just not worth it.

(Matthew 24:13NKJV) But the one who endures to the end shall be saved.

We can't give up no matter how easy giving up is. While enduring is more rewarding, it's going to take some work. You may even fall but get up, steady your course and get back into the race, because it's not over until God says it's over. We sometimes want to end it, but we have to see that God is a forgiving God. So we can't take for granted his grace and mercies, which are fresh and new every morning. Whatever happened last week, yesterday, or even five minutes ago is your past. Repent and turn from your sin and build up your endurance, as a runner builds up there endurance by running they don't sit there and cry about where they want to be, they work daily at getting there. If you want to come out of your situation don't sit there and complain about where you want to be, start activating your faith. Get up every day and begin your day with a declaration of who you are and who you shall be today, give God the praise for it's already being done, and then govern your actions throughout the day. Watch what you say, be mindful of the places you go, seek peace and pursue it, don't set up your own demise prepare but daily for victory. If somewhere throughout your day you come short and fall to temptation, don't beat your self up. Ask God to forgive you and try harder tomorrow. Now that doesn't give you the golden ticket to keep fallen, *for the word says a soul that continues to sin never knew God. (1John 3:6)* You must make it your business to hold fast to your declaration. If you keep fallen into sexual sins I dare you to declare no more! Your body is the temple of the Holy Spirit and I urge you not to violate his temple. After you've made up your mind with a determination not to fall, when you get into that compromising position I dare you to flee from that temptation. Get out of there don't stay there thinking you are strong enough to resist the devil. The bible says to *first submit yourself to God, then resist the devil and he will flee. (James 4:7 NKJV)* If your mind set is set on having sex let me assure you your body is set to follow your thoughts, therefore it is not submitted to God, it is in total submission to the flesh. So for you to stay there thinking you can resist it, is straight crazy because you must first be submitted unto God. Even superman knew that when a situation happened, he couldn't fight it in his suit and tie; he had to run and get outfitted rightly to bring his enemies under subjection. So when a situation is getting the best of you run and get suited up in your most Holy faith by putting on the full armor of God. That you can withstand the wiles of the enemy and then make it your business to get dressed and stay dressed everyday. It's strategic to get dressed before you ever get in a situation, but it's haphazard to wait until it is upon you. (Let's not tempt God Ok!)

Knowing who you are is a strategy that brings forth great fire-power or endurance, because when you know who you are you always have something to come back and defeat the enemy with. He can't speak in your ear and tell you that you are worthless because you know that your worth is great, having been bought with a price and that price being the blood of Jesus.

I am reminded of the wall of endurance. You may ask, what in the world is the wall of endurance? I never read about that in the Bible, Well let me tell you about this wall, this wall has saved my life and is still saving my life. One day, while in prayer, God begin to speak to me about Nehemiah rebuilding the wall that others said could not be built. Even when those who did not believe seen the wall being rebuilt, they begin to offer there services, but with a wrong motive. But with a determination, Nehemiah continued to build with his sword on his side, symbolizing that he was ready to fight for the will of the Father being done. Oh Glory! Grab hold we're going somewhere with this. So in my time of communion with the Lord, God begin to instruct me to go out and purchase enough poster board to cover my corner wall in my dining room. He showed me that I was to cover the wall with this poster board and then label it as the wall of endurance. I was then reminded of the scripture *(Habakkuk 2:2-4 NKJV) and **it says***; *then the Lord answered me and said; write the vision and make it plain on tablets, that he may run who reads it. For the vision is yet for an appointed time; but at the end it will speak, and it will not lie. Though it tarries, wait for it; because it will surely come, it will not tarry. Behold the proud, his soul is not upright in him; but the just shall live by his faith"*

So the instructions the Lord gave me concerning this wall were: every time the enemy or my situation would speak to me something negative, trying to tear me down or make me feel hopeless, I had to go to this wall and begin to write what God says about me and where I'm going in Him! This was to be considered as my faith so that, that which I wrote, God began to challenge me through his word to walk as though it was already so. By turning a deaf ear to the enemy and his accusations, now like Nehemiah I had to become determined to see the will of the Father come forth. I had to keep my sword at my side and keep building, so when the enemy start trying to touch my flesh at night and tell me that I'm lonely and need companionship, I had to be willing to get out my bed, go downstairs to the wall and write that my body is the temple of the Holy Spirit and that I shall not defile the temple, and I will not gratify the lust of my flesh. When my bills where due and there didn't seem to be enough money I had to go to the wall and make it plain that my God shall supply all my needs according to his riches in glory by Christ Jesus! See you have to realize that this wall has and still is saving my life not because there is any power in the wall but because, the just shall live by faith. Faith is the substance of things hoped for and the evidence of things not yet seen. Even though I can't see my way out, I trust in the Lord with all my heart and I lean not unto my own understanding, but in all my ways I acknowledge him and he directs my path. Therefore my faith speaks to that situation because my faith is not in agreement with what the situation is saying but what God says about it He will bring it to pass. As God challenged me to build this wall of endurance, I challenge you to build a wall of endurance to begin to defeat the enemy. So when he tries to speak or do something negative in your life, I dare you to counteract his words with that of faith. I'm declaring deliverance and even now I sense in my spirit that hearts are being lifted, someone is receiving hope where it looked hopeless, someone is regaining their endurance, where the enemy tried to snatch someone's children I'm decreeing that someone is taking this challenge and fighting back. See, what you have to know and understand, is that you have been gifted to speak. It was a gift given to you when you received the Holy Spirit and that's why the enemy would love to keep you quiet about your situation, because he knows that if you ever start talking with the authority invested in you by Christ Jesus he has to back up and bow down and take his hands off of that which was given to you by the Lord. Oh people of God I dare you today to take the challenge, of taking your rightful position and defeating the enemy through your faith

Chapter Three

Security

Security is the state of being secure, by protection or precaution. Yes it's also about being financially set, but is not the security in which I'm talking about. Security is when there is no struggle in your heart or in your emotions because you know that the one who holds your heart holds it with the intent to protect, and the one that strokes your emotions doesn't stroke them for their own pleasure. This is why today we have so many young baby moms and young baby

Daddies, because there is no one to teach these young people about the security that can either make or break them. We wouldn't have so many single moms if these men didn't have such a spirit of manipulation. I guarantee, if these men went to these women and were honest and truthful showing their true colors, most women wouldn't fall at the mercy of their games. Just picture it a guy sees this girl she's beautiful, he wants to hit, but don't really want to commit, so he walks up to her and says "Yo! I think your beautiful I wanna be wit you, I have another girl on the side I haven't been faithful to her and I really don't want to be faithful to you. I just want to be wit you for one night, And if through our carelessness you get pregnant, I'm gonna deny ever being wit you and then when you get all emotionally attached I'm gonna play you for your friend whose had her eye on me for some time. I consider myself a playa', I don't have a real job I hustle because I'm too lazy to get a real 9 to 5, so after you have the baby I won't be there to help raise him anyway cause I'll be locked down just for a little while. But after I get out and because your self esteem fell so low because of how I treated you, I'm gonna sleep wit you a few more times cause in your eyes you'll see me as a star, and I still won't be there for your baby cause if you would sleep with me that easy who else could get you? It's probably my boys seed, and I'll never take you out, cause I can't take the risk of my main girl seein' us together, but yo for real because you are so cute, if you get on welfare, get your own spot in the projects and let me live wit you from time to time I can hold you down. You get a job take care of the bills and your kid and I'll be there to play house. You know I can come home after hittin' the streets, you can have my food on the table and keep the house clean while I play the play station, smoke a blunt wit my boys and then later on we might argue a little because your tired of just being a "live-in" girl friend you want me to make you wifey. But I won't sweat it "cause" I told you from the gate I thought you were beautiful and I just wanted to hit once it's you who got all attached! Ladies this is the scenario that is happening everyday but without the truth being told up front. Some of you reading this book right now are going through or have been through this or similar, but I come to tell you that you can find security or protection. You may ask the question "What can I do? My heart has already been broken, my life is shattered I have kids out of wedlock and they have different dad's, I'm broken and I know I'm worth more but I just can't seem to get up."

(Jeremiah 29:11 NKJV) God has a plan for you and he wants to bring you out of the captivity of your mind, but sometimes our situations dictate to us and where we were so ambitious at one time, we draw back and lose our way. There is a young woman reading this book right now that had goals and dreams and seen a bigger picture for your life, but somewhere along the way you lost your direction, and since you lost it life hasn't been the same. Yes, God sees your tears and he only reveals your inner thoughts because he wants to see you free just as bad, and even greater than what you want. Let me tell you, your heart can be secured, your mind can be secured for all is not lost! Give your life to Jesus; I am a witness he can secure you. Even when I thought I was going to lose my mind my heart was broken defeated thoughts kept running through my head, but when I let Jesus in, he didn't just come in with all the do's and don'ts which Religious folks usually give you, but he came with a plan. A blue print tailor made for me, bringing order to my emotions, soundness to my mind and he

drew close to me and let me draw close to him. God wants to show you a better way, but will you dare turn your back on the world. You tried everything else, but now will you try God? He's calling you passionately by name to walk intimately with him, but will you just answer his call, just say YES!

Parents it is a must that we be the good role model for our children young men will treat these women with respect if we as the mother's will set the example of what a women should and should not except in our lives, and by showing our daughters how not to just settle for anything. Father's if you were upright men to discipline your sons in how to treat the women as a weaker vessel, but to love her like you love your own flesh our boys would think twice. If there were more fathers in the home, young women would set a standard according to how their father entreated them. WE HAVE TO GET IT TOGETHER.

Chapter Four

Defeating Procrastination

Procrastination is one of the biggest reason as to why some don't walk in their promised place. some would like to believe that it's because God doesn't want us to have it or do it yet, when in his word he says; *I Would that you would prosper and be in good health even as your soul prospers (3John:2NKJV)*

Yes there is a time and season for all things, but we have to make sure we are ready in season and out of season. Procrastination is putting off for tomorrow that which we can do today.

The greatest excuse we as human beings like to use is, "I just didn't have time to do it," but when it's something we really want to we certainly make time to do it, we sometimes make the biggest sacrifice if necessary. I can remember in the first years of my battle with Multiple Sclerosis, I would fall paralyzed often. But what didn't change and I wouldn't let change, was that I was in charge of the praise and worship team and I was also an elder in the church. I had responsibilities unto the Lord to usher in his presence and to rule well according to his word, and I refused to let the devil get the best of me. I made it my business to be at every service, and every meeting, but there was one time I was getting ready for a Friday night service, and suddenly I lost all mobility in my legs. Laying on the floor I cried but then I got angry with the devil and I began to army crawl to my closet and get dressed the whole time I kept saying that if I can just get to the house of God I know I will be healed. After I was dressed my father helped me to the car and drove me there. Because of my determination, the paralysis which usually happened for twelve hours began to be released and before I knew it I was up leading praise and worship giving God the praise. Don't get me wrong there was always a praise on my lips from the time I came through the doors, but the difference was I was on my feet walking to and fro giving God the praise. Now I told this story to say this, it really gets me when people say they can't make it to church, or do what God asks of them, because of small things. It's not that they can't they let their body and other decisions dictate it for them. By no means am I saying be like me, but when I seen that healing came because of my press, it made me press even the more. In all things, giving up is not an option. Paul said follow me as I follow Christ and all of us have our moments when we just want to lay around and do nothing, but now is not the time. Jesus is soon to return and the harvest is ripe, but the laborers are few. People of God I urge you to defeat procrastination, by getting up, getting out, and getting busy in the things of God. No more slacking, and that's in every area of your life. If your sink is full of dishes and you're lying around watching T.V., get up, get out there, and get busy. Now is the time to get focus or else you will find yourself in lack, needlessly, looking for someone else to do the work for you. I am learning that mobility, fire-power, and security, can only be activated and stay activated if you first defeat procrastination. The enemy wants you to think that you got all the time in the world, but that is not the case. Time is running out and we are soon to meet the savior face to face. I am reminded of the scripture in *(Matthew 25NKJV)* **speaking of,** *the ten virgins five where wise and five where foolish the five where wise had oil in there lanterns as they went out to meet the bridegroom as well as extra oil, but the foolish only had only the oil that was in their lamps as they also went out to meet the bridegroom, as they went out the bridegroom was delayed in his coming so the ten virgins rested while waiting then they heard a cry saying behold the bridegroom is coming go out to meet him, then all the virgins arose and trimmed their lamps; and the foolish said to the wise, give us some of your oil for our lamps are going out, but the wise answered saying no lest there should not be enough for us and you, but go rather to those who sell and buy for yourselves, and while they went the bridegroom came, and those who were ready went in with him to the wedding and the door was shut.*

I am writing to encourage us as the people of God, to "get right church and let's go home! We don't know the time or place when Jesus will return, but be sure HE IS COMING!!!!! Will you be ready, will you defeat procrastination. Take an evaluation of yourself, turn from your wicked ways, repent of your sins and get busy doing the things of God. Don't let procrastination defeat you.

Chapter Five

Strategy of a single mom

There is a strategy to being a single mother. Yes, even though some think it's just having a baby daddy and collecting a child support check, to some that is the strategy. That is why you have so many disrespectful children running around now. The **Bible says;** *train up a child in the way he should go that when he gets older he will not depart from it (Proverbs 22:6NKJV)*

In the Hebrew text the word train is translated from the word "chahak" (khaw-nak) which means to discipline, dedicate, train-up. It also has the meaning to narrow, throttle or choke, but for the sake of the children we are going to train through discipline and dedication, say glory children!!!!!!! One thing I have come to find out in raising my ten year old son is that regardless of what you tell them if they see contrary from you they are going to do that which you say for them not to do.

Like any other human being, children are visual that is why we must be careful in what atmosphere we place our children into. If your child is constantly in a partying atmosphere with drinking, smoking (cigarettes or wacky tobacco "aka" weed), then you can be sure that when they get older that will be their life style of choice because you trained them up in the way they should go. So mothers ask yourselves, how am I training up my child? A lot of parents have gotten away from disciplining there children. They want to be their friend more so than their parent, and it's time out for that. If we don't discipline them now we will lose them later. As a matter of fact, if we do not discipline them we do not love them! There's no way in the world that I can idly stand by and watch my own flesh and blood going down the wrong path and I do nothing about it. If that was to happen I am saying that I did not love them enough to help them get on the right path. So in being a single mom, it is our responsibility to teach our children the right way, and my friend, I tell you, that Jesus is the only way. The only way you can become a teacher of the word is if you first become a doer of the word once you learn to live his word it will come easy to teach your children his word, and with you living it and then teaching it the children will take heed. Children glean from their parents, so keep this in mind: moving with a plan is moving strategically, but moving without a plan is living dangerously, leaving room for the enemy to destroy. Now I know you struggle sometime and it gets hard, and sometimes you just wish you had some help, how do I know? I've been there and some of you really go through because unlike me you don't just have one child, you have two, three, and some four and more, girl pump your brakes. You can't do this alone, let God in. He will bring that right man in your life, but He wants you to love yourself first. A lot of women say that they are ready to be married, but they continue to try and find the right man, *but the bible says, that when a man finds a wife he finds a good thing and obtains favor with the Lord (proverbs 18:22NKJV)*

My sister, if you can just wait on the Lord things will work out for you, but the first step is to love yourself. A man alone will not complete you, but Christ alone will, and when that man comes along he will be a bonus, adding to your life and not taking away. If you can't do it for yourself, do it for your child/children. They deserve a firm foundation. Children are like arrows in the hands of a mighty man, so whatever direction they are shot in you can be sure that's where they will land. Ladies I know sometimes it seems rough but you can make it. Just don't give up, stay encouraged, and keep fighting, for God has an expected end to your situation. Give him a chance, I found him to be a great husband, and he will bring your whole life into order. You tried everything else now try God.

Chapter Six

Letting Him Find Me

Sometimes letting go is the hardest thing to do, letting go of your plans, your way of thinking and most importantly your pride. Since we were young, we as women, have thought about being married and having children, and what it would feel like to be with someone who loves us for us. But what happens when things don't go as planned? Life in Christ, is about letting go of what you think is right and letting God have his way. (*Jeremiah 29:11NKJV*) *says, for I know the thoughts I have towards you says the Lord plans for good and not evil plans to give you a hope and a future.*

My motto has always been "I can see down the road, but God sees down the road and around the corner. He sees what's coming. So even though it looks good to my eyes, I must still rely on God to show me the whole picture. We can't get impatient or else we find ourselves in a place of offense, not where we are offended, but to where we offend God. When we offend God, we put ourselves in a place of danger that consists of hell's flames. *But they that wait on the Lord you shall renew their strength, they shall mount up on wings as of eagles and soar, and they shall run and not be weary they shall walk and not faint (Isaiah 40:31NKJV).* Letting go is hard to do, but waiting is even harder, It gets easier when you put into perspective what you can and will miss out on, if you choose not to wait. In my waiting, I find that my emotions want to dictate to me to give up, but one thing that I made up in my mind is that giving up is not an option. Yes I made so many mistakes in my life, mistakes that God should have turned his back on me for, but because He is so faithful, He picked me up and dusted me off, giving me another chance to run this race with patience, so that I can still be in the running for the prize; which gives me opportunity, to lay hold to the salvation that brings forth eternal life. " Thank You Father for your grace and your mercy, and for keeping me I love and adore You, Your worthy of my praise you didn't have to, But for your name sake you did and I Bless your holy name" Hallelujah!!!!!!! Settling is not an option, people of God. Before I would be with just anyone for companionship I would be alone. I have too much to lose to just play house! Baby you got to remember this that if a man wants to just live with you and get you pregnant to call himself a man, you got to know that playing house is not a man's game. A real man's game is called commitment and taking on responsibility, loving you for you, and loving you the way he loves his own flesh. Whatever it takes, do not settle you are worth so much more.

The bible says; *when a man finds a WIFE he finds a good thing and obtains favor with the Lord. (Proverbs 18:22NKJV)* **Notice it says when HE finds a wife, not a girlfriend or a significant other, but he has to find a wife. It's him ladies that has to find you, not you find him because he's cute or has a good job. Yes you have standards and don't just let anyone in, but he must be someone that adds to you, taking nothing away from your life. See if you go out and find him and he yields to you because of how cute you are or what you are giving up then baby girl there is another female that can find him And give up the same thing you give up before marriage.**

That is why you have so many silly women fighting over men, because the man has no vision and all he can see is what's hanging before him. Then here you come flaunting your body, and because he's a weak man with no vision he bites at the bate you throw out. You think you found your soul mate, but he knows he got milk without buying the heifer, so while you're expecting him to be faithful he's looking for the next public heifer, because his vision doesn't reach any further than between his legs. Let me encourage you ladies, know that there are good men left with great vision True men of God are not looking for a girlfriend, but we have to allow God to prepare us to be a wife and not just settle for being a girlfriend. When you know who you are, you refuse to accept anything or just give into anything, because a real man doesn't just want casual sex and won't stand for his flesh to be satisfied over his spirit.

We can't keep thinking that if a man has sex with us that means he loves us, in thinking like this we set ourselves up for the fall. We must correct our thinking for, it's not that he loves us, sex is a release and once a man with no vision gets a release he can keep moving on to the next release station if yours close down. Let him know your heart, and don't you give up anything else. I once had an elder tell me "you must be a peach out of reach!" I say, be a peach out of reach and let him drool. If a man drools over you because of how you presented yourself as a whole women and can see how sweet you are without ever tasting, be sure he will commit to you whole heartedly to obtain you for himself, and if you are truly sweet on the inside the way you presented yourself on the outside, he won't go anywhere. Be a wife and not a public heifer!!!!!!! If he doesn't want to marry you with God's intentions, he can't qualify for the goods AMEN?

28

Chapter Seven

The Weapon of Blood

I want to speak to you about the redemptive blood of Jesus Christ, and I want to share with you how someone who has once sinned through fornication, lying, cheating, drunkenness and more can stand before you today forgiven, full of power, and anointed for purpose, all because of the blood of Jesus. *(Matthew 26:28NKJV) for this is my blood of the new covenant, which is shed for many for the remission of sins*

This scripture in brief was the Lords supper being instituted

(Matthew 26:26-27NKJV) And as they were eating Jesus took bread, blessed and broke it, and gave it to the disciples and said, take, eat, this is my body

Then he took the cup, and gave thanks, and gave it to them, saying drink from it all of you

Jesus wanted his disciples to do this in remembrance of what he was getting ready to do for them for he had not yet been crucified. When Jesus was later crucified on the cross, his blood that was shed was for the purpose of us being reconciled to his Father, thus returning to harmony, with God and making us compatible, which gives us a right to the tree of life. See no other blood could be shed for this purpose, not a goat, not a ram, because there is no power in that blood. But when the Lamb of God was slain, the captive (you and I) had a right to be made free. The curtain leading into the holies of holies (which was where the presence of God dwelt) was then ripped from top to the bottom, giving us access to come to God for ourselves. No longer did a priest have to come to God for us. We can now repent for our sins, turn from them, and have eternal life, all because of the precious blood of the Lamb. Now the word remission in its meaning is forgiveness. Oh to be forgiven! Sometimes people even in the church have a way of holding things over your head, but because of the blood that was shed on Calvary's cross we have been reconciled back to the Father, bringing forth remission of our sins, if we repent and turn from our sins. God said that he would take our sins and throw them into the sea of forgetfulness. He won't remember them no more until we do. So ask yourself, what can really put God in remembrance of a sin that he has forgiven? If he's not like man it can't be because it just ran through His mind. God doesn't sit there and say "Oh I remember when Amy sinned against me, that girls going down! No it's when the sin is repeated we literally throw our sins back up in His face. Now you may ask, why we as the human race was out of harmony with God since Jesus shed his blood to reconcile us back to the Father? What knocked us out of harmony? I'm glad you asked, see Adam was the first of the human race setting the tone for all of us and because of his fall, by following Eve, he opened up all of us to iniquity, Adam and Eve literally multiplied evil upon the earth through their disobedience, so in all actuality we where all destined to hell, but God sent his son, who came from heaven to earth to set the example of holiness, and from the earth to the cross to redeem us from the fall of Adam and to forgive us, giving us a right to the tree of life. He literally paid my debt of sin with his blood, from the cross to the grave; so that the sting of death would be removed giving us who believe victory over death that the grave would be conquered. Then he went from the grave to the sky to sit at the right hand of the Father making Intercession for us, and daily preparing a place that one day we would be with him in paradise......GLORY!!!!!!!

I entitled this chapter, the weapon of Blood, because nothing but the Blood of Jesus can wash away my sin! See all have sin and come short of the glory of God, but it is by his blood that we are made whole again. His blood cleanses, protects, and covers us, so think about it, if I confess the blood of Jesus as a protection over my children, I don't care what situation arises the blood will protect them. In *(Exodus 12:23NKJV)* God was getting ready to bring forth a judgment to the Egyptians, so he instructed the

Israelites to apply the blood of the Passover lamb over the doorpost, for the blood of Jesus had not yet been shed. This was to be done for the protection of their children, for God was allowing the first born of the Egyptians to be taken out because of Pharaoh's disobedience to the instruction given, to let the people of God go. So when this was done, and the judgment had befallen them the Israelite's children where not smitten, for the blood of the Passover lamb represented the protection ordained of God through the blood. You have to realize that in order for the power in the blood to work for you, you must be washed in the blood. You must be redeemed by the blood confessing the blood over your life daily, and not just confessing it but living worthy of it. If we were reconciling, it means we are now compatible with God.

That means that if we wash ourselves in the blood of the lamb, God will recognize us as sons simply because we live like His Son, talk like His Son, and carry ourselves in the ordinance of Son ship, qualifying us for eternal life. Do you look like a son? See everyone wants to go to heaven, but will you dare sell out and lose your identity to gain the identity of Christ that you may be accepted by God? There is only one way to get to God, and that is through His Son He sees one way and that is the perfect way that Jesus already made for us. People would like for you to believe that there is more than one way to get to God, but you should not believe that lie *(John 14:6NKJV) Jesus said to him I am the way, the truth, and the life. No one comes to the father except through me.*

He goes on to say if you have seen me you have seen the Father, because Jesus was about the father's business. He came to this earth as an ambassador of heaven saying the way is so plain a fool cannot error. This leaves us with no excuse not to continue on in this race! If you fall get back up quickly, repent of your sins, turn from them and keep running with endurance, for if you endure to the end you shall be saved.

(Luke 22:28NKJV) But you are those who have continued with me in my trials

This small verse was talking about the trials that Jesus faced, which we too are facing as he did in his life and ministry. Jesus experienced temptation *(Luke 4:1-3NKJV)*, he experienced hardships *(Luke 9:58NKJV)*, sorrows *(Luke 19:41NKJV)*, and agony, *(v. 44NKJV)* not to mention the sufferings of the cross, which he knew were yet to come, but he did not give up. We are to mark the perfect man, and even though we come short sometime, dust yourself off and try again with all sincerity. The blood of Jesus was shed that you and I could overcome temptations, hardships, sorrow, and

agony and not be overtaken by these things, so if you find yourself being overtaken, activate your weapon that is the blood of Jesus the Christ, for it reaches to the highest mountain, and it flows through the lowest valley, oh the Blood that gives me strength from day to day will never lose its power!!!!!!!

Chapter Eight

Strategy in my finances

This strategy in being a young single mother was one that took me the longest to grasp. Lets just be real ladies, we love to shop. What God begin to show me is that once we buy something and leave the store, it instantly begins to depreciate quickly losing all of its value. The more we wear it, the more worn out it becomes. Now that's not saying we have to give up shopping all together, it's just that we have to use strategy as we do it. I know some girls who are all about Gucci, Chanel, Roca wear, Baby Phat, They keep their nails done, hair weaved up, toting Dooney and Burke purses, but their house's are not kept, their kids are rebellious, and there's never food in the cabinet or in the fridge. They would rather stop at McDonald's for dinner then prepare a home cooked meal, their lights are being cut off, their home life is in shambles, but they always look good.

When they step foot in the club heads turn, but the problem is, when you would rather look good to obtain praises from everyone else and neglect building up your inheritance, you miss out on the riches that God said you can have. Instantly when I said riches someone's mind went to ridin' on 24's, and a crib wit fifty doors. Yes God desires that you would prosper, but the way we look at money is "I got to get more," but God looks at it like "Yes I Got money but there are bigger things to be had in me."

So the strategy that God showed me, is to first, continue to pay my tithes and offering, then spend my money on things that would build my home and leave an inheritance for my child knowing that a stable home makes for an environment of success. Saving is also a strategy. When you know that something is coming up start adding a little extra to your savings. This is a principle that is simple common sense, but because I thought it to be harder than what it was, it became a struggle. Once you grab hold to using strategy in your finances, you will find yourself cooking instead of eating out all the time, you won't be spending recklessly but you will spend with strategy. Start planning ahead, look forward and don't just spend for today.

Your savings should consist of your children, whether you have them or not. If you see yourself married in the future or just a single career person, every little bit you put a way now will help you in the long run, but we sometimes don't look that far ahead. We want everything now, but if we despise the day of small things, we will not see the end result in success. I am reminded of the scripture in

(Zechariah 4:9-10NKJV) **Even though the temple was being rebuilt some were discouraged because it was smaller than that of Solomon's temple, but the Lord had announced that His pleasure was on this work and that His eye's where watching over it and taking pleasure in it. As it was being completed, He told them in so many words not to despise that which pleases God, so even though it looked small in stature, God was pleased and because of his pleasure in it He blessed it. So I tell you as you function in your finances, first, by giving God that which is His and then, move strategically bringing order to your life, God will bless it and that which is little becomes much but only when it's put in the Master's hands. The biggest test to overcome in this is, to put your flesh under subjection. Loosen self control even when those boots are sitting on the shelf half priced, calling your name. While that light bill is due, weigh it out in your mind: What good is it for me, to buy these boots and be sitting in the dark tomorrow. "Wisdom cry's out loud," but will you have enough common sense to obey it?**

Chapter Nine

Overcoming Multiple Sclerosis

Six years is a long time, but boy did it teach me to trust in the Lord with all my heart and lean not unto my own understanding. At the age of 25 I was diagnosed with Multiple Sclerosis also known a M.S., a disease in which attacks the immune system as well as the nervous system Multiple Sclerosis causes blindness, paralysis, weakness, and numbness, you name it, I had it. I can remember in 2003 I was going back to school to finish my education for Cosmetology and a few weeks before school, I started getting numbness on my left side, and I remember thinking "how in the world am I going to be able to cut hair? I can barely fill anything in my left hand." I later went to take a bath placing my left leg in the tub and all was well, but when I placed my right leg in I can remember being burned because the water was too hot, but I never felt it because my legs where losing feeling. Even though I was experiencing this I never went to the hospital, thinking whatever this is it will clear up. I was an aerobics instructor and I would ride my bike for three miles everyday. I felt I was in the best shape of my life, but how many of you know that just when you think that all is well God is like it's time to go higher and then comes the trials. Before this all began, I can remember getting a word that, like Job God, was pleased with me and He was bragging on me and for me to be encouraged. At that time I had no idea what it all entailed. I went on to school and got my education. I took one of two state exams and passed it with flying colors, but the second test I never took because the numbness started again, and this time it was followed by headaches and an imbalanced equilibrium, so at any point I would go from a standing position to picking myself up off the floor. From that point on things just kept getting worse, I would still try to ride my bike thinking all I had to do was build up my strength and all would go well, but that theory didn't work. Soon riding my bike became a battle that I was slowly losing. One day as I was riding my bike with my son, my hands went numb while riding down a hill which had a busy street at its end. My hands instantly became too weak to pull back my brake and I went flying at neck breaking speed down this hill. In fear for my son and myself, I began to call to him to keep pumping his brakes while he was yelling "mommy" As I drifted further and further away from him, I started yelling the name that is above every name, "JESUS, JESUS, HELP ME JESUS!" As I was coming to the street, just then my bike came to a complete stop just inches from the street and moments later my son stopped right beside me, I didn't care who was looking at me, I had to give God some praise! After all that, you would have thought that I got off the bike and pushed it home right? No I was still determined to ride this bike again with the same endurance I had before, so as I went on I seemed to tire so easily and as I was pumping up a hill that I usually took with ease, that hill defeated me like a rookie. Then when my energy was gone uncontrollably I fell off the bike, unable to move, not realizing I was laying in a bunch of broken glass, but by the grace of God I did not sustain one injury. I quickly came to the realization that my riding had to come to an end. With the headaches continuing, I woke up on morning with a film over my right eye and it continued off and on all day. I didn't know what it was, so I rebuked it and kept going throughout my day. We laugh about it now, but that day my mom wanted me to drive her to Pittsburgh, PA, approximately 1 hour and 45 minutes away from our home. I never told her I was having trouble seeing I just kept praying Lord help me make it to my destination and home. Mom didn't find out until the following day when I woke up with my right eye uncontrollably shut, all the straining I did to see the day before became too much and the third nerve in my brain collapsed. I later found that out, because after that experience, I finally went to the doctor just to go through a series of test and be diagnosed with Multiple Sclerosis. I tell you the truth I was in denial for years thinking there was no way, this mess don't even run in my family and I thought the doctors were crazy. I kept praying and standing on the word of the Lord, but be sure I was going through. Now as the years went on I went through spurts of blindness, paralysis and so much more, but I never let go of this conclusion: He was wounded for my transgressions and bruise for my iniquities and the chastisement of my peace was upon him and by his stripes I am healed. Knowing who you are in Christ is a strategy all in its self, why? Because when you know who you are it doesn't matter what comes your way, there's no devil in hell that can change the way you see yourself in Christ. I remember one time when I could barely walk and someone asked me why don't you go and get a handicap sticker and I look them right in the face and told them "because I'm not handicapped," and they looked at me like "can't she see that she can't walk" *(Proverbs 23:7NKJV) For as he thinketh in his heart, so is he.*

If my thought process became that of one who is defeated, then that's what I would have been, but because I seen this as something temporal, that's what it was.

Now don't get me wrong, I am still overcoming Multiple Sclerosis, but when I look back from where God has brought me from to where I am now, I can say with confidence that I am healed. The Doctors told me in the beginning that the disease was progressing so fast, that within six months I would be confounded to a wheel chair unable to feed myself. Now in six years I can say I never had to use a wheelchair, I used a walker once while in the hospital after an exacerbation which took out my mobility. Even then the Doctor told me that I would have to use a walker when I went home and I told the

Doc "I'm not using no walker" in joking fun I told him "I was too cute to use a walker" He laughed and said "Well I'm going to send you home with a prescription for the walker," I said "that's fine, but I'm not going to need it." And one year later on the exact date that they gave me the prescription I pulled it out and begin to show people saying "Look what the Lord has done," Oh GLORY I never had to use the walker outside of the hospital. I declared what God's word says and sure enough he established it, for it is his job to establish it! Some plant, some water but it is God who gives the increase and what is increase? To make large, and when it's made large it is done to make it be seen. So now because God gave the increase it is evident that God is the God that healed me! Every time they would put me on medicine the effects the doctors said were rare side effects, were the first things that happened to me being on the medicine, why? Because God won't share his glory with no man! No doctor with his medicine can say that it's because of the medicine that I am standing healed today, but it is by the grace and mercy of Jesus Christ through the power of his blood, that I, Sarina Donyell Hardison am healed Thank You Jesus!!!!!!

Chapter Ten

A Work in Progress

Believe it or not people, there is a strategy to being a work in progress, and that strategy is diligence, being determined to make it to the end no matter what comes your way, *(Matthew 24:13NKJV) says, but he that endures to the end shall be saved*

God has an expected end for your situation. That is a promise you can take to the bank, but remember how we live will determine our end. Yes your going to fall, but don't use that as an excuse to stay down or to continue to sin, strive towards holiness and if someone else falls around you don't judge, consider yourself, unless you also be tempted. If you see your brother overtaken in a fault ye which are spiritual, restore that one with a spirit of meekness *(Galatians 6:1NKJV)*. Oh my brother, my sister if you find yourself in a fallen state right now, I dare you to get up repent and turn from those ways and seek the Lord while he yet may be found. There's coming a time very soon that Jesus will return for his bride (believers) and Satan will reek havoc on this earth, and we who endured will be snatched out of here before this occurs but them that remain will suffer great persecution just for mentioning the name Jesus, I hear so many people say I will give my life to Christ one day, but not right now I'm too young. Well I say, you can bow your knee now and give your heart to Jesus or you can wait until the day when he can not be found and bow your knee then, but one day every knee will bow and every tongue will confess that Jesus is Lord. Think about it what is so good about your situation that you can't let it go and turn to the Lord? For every good thing you just mentioned, I hope it was good enough to hear the words depart from me you worker of iniquity I never knew you, just to spend eternity in total damnation! People of God I love you and by no means am I telling you all this stuff and not evaluating myself, I too have to give an account for all the things I have done, but one thing you can be sure of, is that regardless of all I been through I choose right now while there is breath in my body and life in my soul, to live everyday of my life in total reverence to Jesus Christ whether I lose friends, family or whoever, as for me and my house we will serve the Lord. I am reminded of a time when our ministry had a tent revival and a young man came and gave his life to the Lord, and at that moment he vowed to serve the Lord with his whole heart. We encouraged him to come fellowship and be taught the word of God, and with great joy in his eyes he said he would be there, but just when he left us the lifestyle of the streets begin to call to him again and he answered. No one could find him until one day I seen him at a convenient store, and as I was going in and he was coming out, I instantly stopped and begin to talk to him letting him know that we were looking for him and was excited about him coming to fellowship with us. Just then he looked me in the eyes and said "You know, I think I made a mistake by getting saved that night, I'm not ready, I'm young, I have my whole life ahead of me, I'll get saved one day but not now, my heart dropped as I begin to tell him about the power of Jesus and how tomorrow is not promised to him, he grabbed me by the hand and said "I know I'm just not ready" and walked away. I cried out for this young man that God would soften his heart, but a few days later as I watched the news, they broadcast that this young man was shot and killed in the hallway of his apartment building, I cried and cried and cried, because this young man could have lived a long and prosperous life with Jesus as his Lord and savior, yet he chose to be snuffed out in his 20's, under the influence of the enemy, when I was called to sing at his funeral all I could do prior to singing my song was tell those who remained, the brief experience I had with this gentleman at the convenient store and let them know the importance of them choosing God now. for tomorrow is not promised to them. Please I beg of you to hear the voice of the Lord for you don't know if this is the last call for your life, and why chance it? Some of you reading this book right now, someone has spoke to you on numerous occasions about changing your life and giving it over to Jesus, and you have turned a deaf ear because you thought you would be missing something if you gave your life to Jesus or if you gave up those friends, but let me tell you beloved, God is not going to bid you to come much longer, he said in his word he will not strive with man always, so I encourage you to seek him while he yet may be found. There's nothing that you have done that he can't forgive, you're not in it too deep. Some of you, it's going to take you changing your realm of friends because these people are so wrapped up in drug dealing and gang bangin', that you just being in there company have a deadline on your life. You literally have to run for your life and if you don't run to the arms of God you will lose your life. I'm sensing this thing in my spirit hard, God can fix it, but you got to surrender there's no time to play. You've heard of STOP, DROP, AND ROLL well that will help you if you're on fire!! If right now you're on fire do that and your chances of being extinguished are better; (laugh baby it's good for your soul)!

But I say;

STOP – sinning

REPENT – to God for your sins

&

TURN – from your old ways and follow Christ to a new you!

This is your day things are going to get better, life is going to get sweeter, I'm not saying that you will never have any problems but what I am saying is that for every temptation God will give you a way of escape LET GO, AND LET GOD HAVE HIS WAY!!!!

You must endure to the end get yourself in fellowship with some believers and stand on His word. If you're in the Johnstown area I can vouch for "Works of Deliverance Fellowship International

Ministries" Located at 550 Park Avenue, Johnstown, Pa 15902.

We love the Lord and are striving to obtain the prize of a high calling. Remember all have sinned and come short of the glory of God, but a righteous man falls seven times but he gets back up again! If you can forgive yourself you can have eternal life, why? Because once you ask God with a sincere heart He forgives you and won't remember it anymore until you do, and you remember it, by repeating it. Be blessed beloved and walk in God's unmerited favor.

A Call to the Laborers

(Matthew 9:37-38)He said to his disciples; the harvest is great, but the workers are few, so pray to the Lord who is in charge of the harvest; ask him to send more workers into his field.

Praise the Lord my brother's and sisters in Christ! I am calling out to you today that you would become so determine to go to the highways and hedges, to compel them that are lost to come home to the loving arms of our savior Jesus Christ! If we take a moment to look around, we will see that the harvest is ripe, but sadly the laborers are few, and now is not the time for us to be tempted or drawn away by our own lust. We must lay aside every weight and sin that does so easily beset us and run this race with patience knowing that some one is out there waiting and anticipating the true sons of God to be revealed. We got to move in this season, because lives must be change and bodies healed by the power of God which was invested in you by Jesus Christ. The enemy is on the hunt to take you out by killing your strength; people are getting so preoccupied, but now is not the time! Jesus told his disciples not to leave Jerusalem until they received the promised gift of the Holy Spirit, and we too we cannot move ahead of him nor can we lag behind. This is a call to the Laborers: Get up! It's time to move! If you have fallen short get up repent and turn someone is depending on the God in you so take your city by storm, be ambassadors of Jesus Christ, and kingdom citizens snatching souls from the very fire of Hell!

May God Bless and Keep You!!

Elder Sarina D. Hardison

Remarks

From Pastor Sabrina A. Hardison;

Sarina I'm very pleased with your diligence, your stamina, and your persistence. I watched how you travailed, and overcame so many obstacles that stood in your way, this you did through the tears and laughter, but through it all, I seen your strength and hope that came forth out of you I am very Godly proud of you. What you're writing about is not just something you heard, but your penmanship is your experience. I have seen God move in your life, keep the faith and keep pressing on there are others following behind you, more than you know.

I love you, mom

From Aletha Triplin;

I'm proud of you and I'm your biggest fan, I see how God has moved in your life, I know that I can do this! So I'm a work in progress!!!!

From Treviaun Hardison;

Mommy I love you and I'm proud of you for finally getting your book done, and I pray that you will write a whole lot more books to teach others about God and I pray that while you're writing all these books that you will stay encouraged because you're a great mom!

From Joy Cox;

Elder Sarina Hardison is an awesome woman of God that He uses mightily! I'm sure this book will be full of wisdom and spiritual insight that will help equip the body of Christ, and take us to the next level!

From Camillya Taylor;

I'm proud of you and I know your going to do great!

From Anna Ellis;

I watched Elder in her physical weakness become strong and healthy, physically and spiritually which helped me overcome my dilemmas I love you, and I'm always praying for you! Aunt Belle

To our dearest sister Sarina;

We are so happy and excited for your great achievement that you worked so hard on. Most people could not reach their goals because of the trials that stand in their way, but thank God for your determination and consistency. Remember this; People have a lot to say, and they feel that they need to be heard, but fail to realize that God has a lot to say, and really need to be heard. So with that being said keep letting God use you. Love Michael and Artrese Taylor

From Cindy Sampson;

Elder, knowing how to find peace in the midst of the storm is critical to our development, and doing it strategically is the key.

May God Bless you in this season!